Communication

Guided/Group Reading Notes

Gold Band

Contents

OXFORD

Introduction

Reading progression in Year 2/Primary 3

In Year 2/P3 children begin to read longer, more challenging and less familiar texts independently. Most children are able to decode new words quickly and automatically, and this helps them build up their pace, fluency and stamina.

The Project X texts at **gold band** are slightly longer than those at purple band but still contain a core of familiar high and medium frequency words and phonically regular words to help build children's confidence as they become independent readers.

Throughout the books, natural-sounding language is used as this encourages readers to use their knowledge of the rhythms and structures of language to support them as they make sense of the text.

Short chapters are introduced and the complexity of character, plot and setting continues to develop, giving many opportunities for inference and deduction as well as recall. Sentence structures become longer and more complex at gold band, so readers will encounter both compound and complex sentences. The full range of punctuation marks is used including speech marks and apostrophes showing contraction and possession.

A range of non-fiction features, including tables, labelled diagrams, captions, bulleted lists, timelines, flow diagrams, quizzes and glossaries, encourage children to read and interpret the information that is presented in a variety of ways.

Visual literacy is supported through additional action and information in the illustrations, the use of graphic devices, cartoon and comic strip genres and the suggestions for visualization comprehension strategies suggested in these note.

Progression in the Project X character books

In *The Thing in the Cupboard*, the children discover the existence of an X-bot in the first of a two-part story. They try to fix the X-bot in *Message in an X-bot*, and through it they receive a message that warns them of the presence of Dr X.

Guided/group reading

The engaging content and careful levelling of the Project X books makes them ideal for use in guided/group reading sessions. The advantages of using guided/group reading, as well as charts to help you assess the appropriate level for a reading group, are discussed in the *Teaching Handbook* for Year 2/P3.

To use the books in guided/group reading sessions, you should select a book at a band that creates a small degree of challenge for the group of pupils. Typically, children should be able to read about 90% of the book unaided. This level of 'readability' provides the context for children to practise their reading and build reading confidence. The 'challenge' in the text provides opportunities for explicitly teaching reading skills.

These *Guided/Group Reading Notes* provide support for each book in the **Communication** cluster, along with suggestions for follow-up activities. Books in the gold band could be covered in one or two guided/group reading sessions.

Speaking, listening and drama

Talk is crucial to learning. Children need plenty of opportunities to express their ideas through talk and drama, and to listen to and watch the ideas of others. These processes are important for building reading engagement, personal response and understanding. Suggestions for speaking, listening and drama are given for every book. Within these *Guided/Group Reading Notes* the speaking and listening activities are linked to the reading assessment focuses.

Building comprehension

Understanding what we have read is at the heart of reading. To help readers become effective in comprehending a text these *Guided/Group Reading Notes* contain practical strategies to develop the following important aspects of comprehension:

- Previewing
- Predicting
- Activating and building prior knowledge
- Questioning
- Recalling
- Visualizing and other sensory responses
- Deducing, inferring and drawing conclusions

- Determining importance
- Synthesizing
- Empathizing
- Summarizing
- Personal response, including adopting a critical stance.

The research basis and rationale for focusing on these aspects of comprehension is given in the *Teaching Handbook* for Year 2/P3.

Reading fluency

Reading fluency combines automatic word recognition, reading with pace, and expression. Rereading, fluency and building comprehension are linked together in a complex interrelationship, where each supports the other. This is discussed more fully in the *Teaching Handbook* for Year 2/P3.

Opportunities for children to read aloud are important in building fluency and reading aloud to children provides models of expressive fluent reading. Suggestions for purposeful and enjoyable oral reading and rereading/re-listening activities are given in the follow-up activities to guided/group reading and in the notes for parents on the inside cover of each book.

The Project X *Interactive Stories* software can be used to provide a model of reading fluency for the whole class and/or opportunities for individuals or small groups of children to listen to stories again and again. Listening to stories being read is particularly effective with EAL children.

Building vocabulary

Explicit work on enriching vocabulary is important in building reading fluency and comprehension. Repeatedly encountering a word and its variants helps it become known on sight. The thematic 'cluster' structure of Project X supports this because words are repeated within and across the books. Suggestions for vocabulary work are included in these notes. The vocabulary chart on pages 10–11 shows when vocabulary is repeated and new words are introduced. It also indicates those words that can be used to support learning alongside a structured phonics and spelling programme.

Developing a thematic approach

Helping children to make links in their learning supports their development as learners. All the books in this cluster have a focus on the theme **Communication**. A chart showing the cross-curricular potential of this theme is given in the *Teaching Handbook* for Year 2/P3, along with a rationale for using thematic approaches. Some suggestions for cross-curricular activities are also given in these notes, in the follow-up suggestions for each book.

In guided/group reading sessions, you will also want to encourage children to make links between the books in the cluster. Grouping books in a cluster allows readers to make links between characters, events and actions across the books. This enables readers to build complex understandings of characters gradually, to give reasons why things happen and how characters may change and develop. It can help them recognize cause and effect. It helps children reflect on the skill of determining importance, as a minor incident or detail in one book may prove to have greater significance when considered across several books.

In the **Communication** cluster, some of the suggested links that can be explored across the books include:

- using codes and ciphers
- making masks (**Art and design**)
- designing robotic toys (**DT**)
- creating Powerpoint presentations with soundtracks (**ICT, Music**).

Reading into writing

The Project X books provide both models and inspiration to support children's writing. Suggestions for relevant, contextualized and interesting writing activities are given in the follow-up activities for each book. These include both short and longer writing opportunities. The activities cover a wide range of writing contexts so writers can develop an understanding of adapting their writing for different audiences and purposes.

The Project X *Interactive Stories* software contains a collection of 'clip art' assets from the character books – characters and settings – that children can use in their writing.

There are also a number of writing frames and activity sheets that can be downloaded and printed for pupils to use, or that pupils can write/type into directly to practise writing and ICT skills.

Selecting follow-up activities

These *Guided/Group Reading Notes* give many ideas for follow-up activities. Some of these can be completed within the reading session. Some are longer activities that will need to be worked on over time. You should select those activities that are most appropriate for your pupils. It is not expected that you would complete all the suggested activities.

Home/school reading

Books used in a guided/group reading session can also be used in home/school reading programmes.

Before a guided/group reading session, the child could:

- read the first chapter or section of a book
- read a related book from the cluster to build background knowledge.

Following a guided/group reading session, the child could:

- reread the book at home to build reading confidence and fluency
- read the next chapter or section in a longer book
- read a related book from the cluster.

Advice for parents on supporting their child with reading at home is provided in the inside covers of individual books. There is further advice for teachers concerning home/school reading partnerships in the *Teaching Handbook* for Year 2/P3.

Assessment

During guided/group reading teachers make ongoing assessments of individuals and of the group. Reading targets are indicated for each book and you should assess against these reading targets. You should select just one or two targets at a time as the focus for the group. The same target can be appropriate for several literacy sessions or over several texts.

Readers should be encouraged to self-assess and peer-assess against the target/s.

Further support for assessing pupils' progress is provided in the *Teaching Handbook* for Year 2/P3.

Continuous reading objectives and ongoing assessment

The following objectives will be supported in *every* guided/group reading session and are therefore a *continuous* focus for attention and assessment. These objectives are not listed in full for each book, but as you listen to individual children reading you should undertake ongoing assessment, against these decoding and encoding objectives:

- Read independently and with increasing fluency longer and less familiar texts **5.1**
- Know how to tackle unfamiliar words that are not completely decodable **5.3**
- Read and spell less common alternative graphemes including trigraphs **5.4**
- Read high and medium frequency words independently and automatically **5.5**

Further objectives are provided as a focus within the notes for each book. Correlation to the specific objectives within the Scottish, Welsh and Northern Ireland curricula are provided in the *Teaching Handbook* for Year 2/P3.

Recording assessment

The assessment chart for the **Communication** cluster is provided on page 48 of the *Teaching Handbook* for Year 2/P3.

Diagnostic assessment

If an individual child is failing to make good progress or he or she seems to have a specific problem with some aspect of reading you will want to undertake a more detailed assessment. Details of how to use running records for diagnostic assessment are given in the *Teaching Handbook* for Year 2/P3.

Vocabulary chart

At Year 2/P3, children should:

- read high and medium frequency words independently and automatically
- read and spell
  - less common alternative graphemes
  - compound words and polysyllabic words
  - suffixes and prefixes.

NB There are too many high frequency words in each book to list them all. The first 100 words are known by this stage. A selection is given from the final 200 words in the *300 common words in order of frequency* list. Examples only are given in each category.

The Thing in the Cupboard	**High frequency words**	thing, laughed, inside, white, around, dark, need, coming, looking
	Phonetically regular compound and polysyllabic words	sulked, pushed, spider, pitch, snorted, gloomy
	Alternative graphemes including trigraphs	wonder, practise, captain, store, crept, invisible, high, leapt, quickly, through, surprise, elephants, herd, noticed, crawled, exclaimed
	Challenge words	cupboard, decided, whispered
Message in an X-bot	**High frequency words**	soon, thinks, small, about, keep, didn't
	Phonetically regular compound and polysyllabic words	robot, chased, evening, computer, broken, impressed, handed, humming, scuttled, deserved
	Alternative graphemes including trigraphs	message, scary, squashed, mystery, mean, pointing, e-mailed, please, hour, half, dials, wrong, lurched, image
	Challenge words	closely, answer, talk

What's on the Box?	High frequency words	place, need, different, going, round, man
	Phonetically regular compound and polysyllabic words	channel, transmits, video, network, cartoon, signal
	Alternative graphemes including trigraphs	audio, communication, satellite, television, station, programme, wondered, location, digital, broadcast, volcanoes
	Challenge words	scientist, technology, audience, knowledge, John Logie Baird, David Attenborough
The Deadly Boomslang	High frequency words	great, along, wanted, river, lived, first, really, gone
	Phonetically regular compound and polysyllabic words	gather, bitten, hunt, catch, stamping, singing, clever, blind, rushing, twittering, hissing, swelling
	Alternative graphemes including trigraphs	stories, tale, leader, dead, someone, woman, speak, muttered, boasted, heart, scaly, sneaky, deadly, noisy, shady, friends, listening, caught, scurrying, knife, noise, heroes
	Challenge words	villagers, knowledge, listened
Let's Play and other things animals say	High frequency words	animals, other, over, food, found, last
	Phonetically regular compound and polysyllabic words	owl, swoops, struts, glands, troops, cackling
	Alternative graphemes including trigraphs	trail, feathers, warning, tough, beautiful, scent, laughing, monkeys, predict, elephant
	Challenge words	chemical, attention, whistle, communicate, dolphin, whale, direction

The Thing in the Cupboard

BY CHRIS POWLING

About this book

Tiger shrinks and goes into the school cupboard. He finds a 'Thing' (an X-bot), but he doesn't know what it is. First of a two-part story continued in *Message in an X-bot*.

You will need

- *Instructions for making a communication device* Photocopy Master 40, *Teaching Handbook* for Year 2/P3
- *Design your own X-bot* Photocopy Master 41, *Teaching Handbook* for Year 2/P3
- A sealed box

	Literacy Framework objective	Target and assessment focus
Speaking, listening, group interaction and drama	○ Tell real and imagined stories using the conventions of familiar story language 1.2	○ We can retell stories using familiar story words such as 'once upon a time', 'meanwhile', etc. **AF2**
Reading See also continuous reading objectives listed on page 9.	○ Use syntax and context to build their store of vocabulary when reading for meaning 7.4 ○ Explore how particular words are used, including words and expressions with similar meanings 7.5	○ We can use syntax and context to build vocabulary as we read for meaning **AF1** ○ We can talk about the language and literary features that the author uses **AF5**

Before reading

*To activate prior knowledge and
encourage prediction*

- Look at the front cover. Ask the children
  what this is a picture of.

- Ask the children to suggest questions
  that the front cover image evokes, e.g.
  I wonder what the thing behind Tiger is?

- Invite them to suggest other stories
  (including those viewed as films) in
  which a watch or something similar is
  used for communication.

- Give the children the opportunity to try different ways of
  getting urgent messages to each other, e.g. walkie-
  talkies, cups on a string, text messages, emails.

*To support decoding and word recognition and introduce
new vocabulary*

- Take a picture walk through the text and let children
  infer what might happen. At the same time, introduce
  some of the new vocabulary that is suggested in the
  vocabulary chart (see page 10). You may want to invite
  them to point out some of the unfamiliar vocabulary,
  and then work with them to decode those words.

To engage readers and model fluent reading

- Read Chapters 1 and 2 to the children. Demonstrate how
  you use your voice to build suspense at key points (e.g.
  when Tiger begins to shrink, when the other children
  realize what he has done).

- Ask if anyone is afraid of spiders. What other things
  are the group afraid of? How do they think Tiger must
  be feeling?

During reading

- Ask the children to read the rest of the book.
- Ask the children what to do if they encounter a difficult word, modelling with an example from the book if necessary. Praise children who successfully decode unfamiliar words.
- Ask them to pay particular attention to how the author uses words to create pictures in their minds, and to note down any words or phrases that particularly help them to imagine the scene.

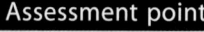

Assessment point

Listen to individual children reading and make ongoing assessments on their approaches to tackling new words and reading fluency. AF1

 After reading

Returning to the text

- Look back to Chapter 3 (*The Thing ...*). How has the author used language and punctuation to build suspense? (**adopting a critical stance**)

- Ask children to share their notes and talk about the different ways the author has created pictures in their minds throughout the story, e.g. use of descriptive words (*dark and gloomy*), use of similes (*like the patter of tiny feet*), use of pauses to build suspense, use of ellipses and repetition of dialogue (*It's a, a*), and use of powerful verbs (*dived, bounced*, etc.) (**adopting a critical stance**)

Assessment point

Can children talk about the language and literary features the author uses? AF5

- Now look at page 13. Why has the author written the word *Meanwhile* in large, bold print? Discuss how the author has used this technique to move the story on, by helping the reader to understand what is going on in a different location. Give children practice in making up oral sequences that use this word, e.g. 'The children were sitting in the class. Meanwhile the teacher was hiding behind the door.' Let them have fun with this word play.

. . . . >

Building comprehension

○ Take children into a large space (e.g. outdoors, the hall). Read up to page 5: *"Shush!" she said. "For today's drama lesson I want you to all to be spiders."* Ask them to imagine they are in that class. Get them to talk to a partner about how they might feel about this. Then get them to assume a freeze-frame position as a response. Once they have assumed their position, tap several children on the shoulder and ask them to tell the group what they are thinking. (**visualizing**, **sensory response**)

- What do they think the Thing is? Where has it come from? How do you think it might affect future stories? Why do they think the watch has a warning for an X-bot? How might this be linked to the Thing? (**deducing, inferring, drawing conclusions**)

- Bring in a sealed box and tell the children it has the Thing in it. Tell them it can hear and understand them. Get them to ask the Thing questions that will help them to find out where it comes from. You could tell them it cannot speak at the moment but perhaps they will receive written answers later on. This can be really fun if you can get another adult to hide and answer the questions (perhaps through a microphone and speakers). (**questioning, building prior knowledge**)

Building vocabulary

- Look at the simile on page 5: *His face was as white as the lines on a football pitch*. Talk about how this is effective. (Not only does it give a clear image of how white Tiger is, it also evokes his personality because he loves football.)

- Get the children to make up similes about themselves or friends that achieve a similar effect, e.g: 'My eyes were as wide as a dinner plate' (for someone who has a hearty appetite); 'She came bouncing into the classroom like a pogo stick'.

Follow-up activities

Writing activities
- Write a short story that includes a 'meanwhile' sentence, paragraph or chapter (depending on ability). Once children have written their stories, give them time to reread the stories to themselves and then tell the stories to the class. (**longer writing task**)
- Using the *Instructions for making a communication device* Photocopy Master, write instructions for making a communication device. (**short writing task**)
- Write a description of themselves or a friend, using similes in the description. (**short writing task**)

Cross-curricular and thematic opportunities
- Design a way of getting an urgent message to a friend on the other side of the playground. (**Science, DT**)
- Complete the *Design your own X-bot* Photocopy Master. (**Art and design**)
- Explore the movement of different animals (e.g. spiders). (**Drama, Dance**)

Message in an X-bot

BY TONY BRADMAN

About this book

Following on from *The Thing in the Cupboard*, the children try to fix the X-bot. Through it, they receive a message that warns them of the presence of Dr X.

You will need

- *The X-bot* Photocopy Master 42, *Teaching Handbook* for Year 2/P3
- *Predictive text spelling game* Photocopy Master 43, *Teaching Handbook* for Year 2/P3

	Literacy Framework objective	**Target and assessment focus**
Speaking, listening, group interaction and drama	○ Present ... their own stories or work drawn from different parts of the curriculum for members of their own class 4.2	○ We can produce a scene from the story for the rest of the class to see AF2
Reading See also continuous reading objectives listed on page 9.	○ Draw together ideas and information from across a whole text, using simple signposts in the text 7.1	○ We can understand the main facts and events in a text and, where appropriate, their sequence AF2

Before reading

To activate prior knowledge and encourage prediction

- Draw the group's attention to the title. What do they think the message might be?

- Now turn to page 2. Ask children to recall the previous story, using the pictures to help. Do they have any thoughts about what the Thing is?

- Knowing what they do about the characters in the story now, ask the children to predict which character Max could ask for help.

To preview the text

- Look at the chapter headings for the first four chapters (but make sure you do not let them see pages 18 and 19 as this would spoil the story). Discuss what the themes might be within each chapter.

To support decoding and word recognition and introduce new vocabulary

- Sit the children around a computer and discuss all the vocabulary they can think of that is linked to electronic devices (e.g. computers, mobile phones). Ask them to become word detectives: to look through the book and collect technical words, e.g. *e-mail*.

During reading

- Ask the children to read the rest of the story. If you have not already done so, remind them of some of the technical vocabulary that they are likely to meet. Praise children who successfully decode unfamiliar words.

- As they read, ask them to note the main points of the story. Encourage them to consider which parts of the story have the most impact on the eventual outcome. (**determining importance**)

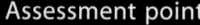

> **Assessment point**
>
> Can children identify the main events of the story? AF2

 After reading

- Ask children to think about what the X-bot is and who Dr X might be. Can they decide whether the X-bot is friend or foe? How do the author and illustrator make you feel that the X-bot is a threat initially? (**inferring**)

- Why does Max decide that Ant deserves to keep the robot? (**inferring**)

- Let the group compare their completed main points notes. Have they all identified the main episodes? Where they have different points of view, discuss the reasons for their decisions, asking them to justify their points of view. (**determining importance**)

Building comprehension

- Ask them to use the pictures to retell the story. (**summarizing**)

- Ask them to create a mind-map of the story. (**synthesizing**)

> **Assessment point**
>
> Can children identify the main parts of the story and sequence the events accurately? AF2

- Can they infer why Max decided that sending pictures to Ant would be most likely to get him to help? **(inferring)**

- Look together at the pictures on pages 22 and 23. Can children discuss the pictures and make predictions about what might happen in future episodes? **(predicting)**

- Go into role as the hologram. Ask the children to generate questions that will help them to find out who the X-bots are, where they have come from and who Dr X may be. **(questioning)**

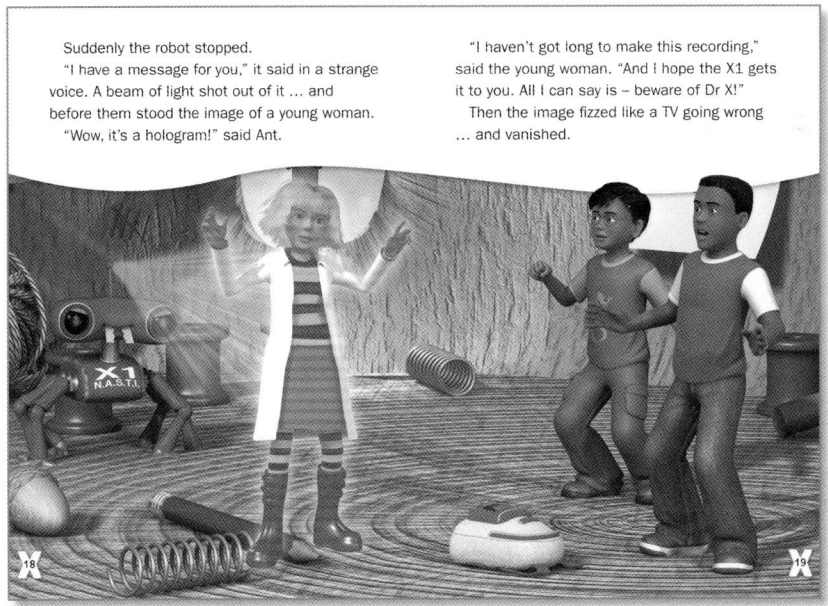

Suddenly the robot stopped.
"I have a message for you," it said in a strange voice. A beam of light shot out of it ... and before them stood the image of a young woman.
"Wow, it's a hologram!" said Ant.

"I haven't got long to make this recording," said the young woman. "And I hope the X1 gets it to you. All I can say is – beware of Dr X!"
Then the image fizzed like a TV going wrong ... and vanished.

- Ask them to try and define the space of the micro-den. Get them to choose part of the classroom and set it up to represent the physical space of the micro-den. (This will help them to imagine the scene as a backdrop for action.) The position of significant places such as entrances or pieces of furniture can be marked. Other information such as what the den smells like, or sounds like, can be agreed before the group goes into role. **(visualizing, synthesizing)**

Building fluency

Ask the children to reread Chapter 4 (*Trapped!*). Give them time to prepare this scene as a dramatic presentation. Ask them questions such as 'How could you recreate ...', to help to visualize the scene. Let them choose or make props. Remind them to think carefully about facial expressions, sound effects, etc. (**visualizing and other sensory responses, empathizing**)

• •>

Building vocabulary

- Give the children *The X-bot* Photocopy Master. Ask them to collect words to put around the X-bot that describe the robot and the special powers it may have.

- Alternatively, give children the *Predictive text spelling game* Photocopy Master.

Follow-up activities

Writing activities

- Compose text messages to friends. Discuss the abbreviations used. (**short writing task**)
- Compose e-mails to friends, pen-pals, etc. (**short writing task**)
- Use the pictures of future events (pages 22 and 23) to write a sequel entitled, 'The characters meet the X-bots'. (**longer writing task**)

Cross-curricular and thematic opportunities

- Bring robotic and remote-controlled toys to school. Explore how they move, how they work, etc. (**DT**)
- Create a design for a robotic toy. (**DT**)
- Draw a plan of the micro-den to scale. (**Maths, Geography**)
- Make some stop-frame animations using remote-controlled toys. (**ICT**)

What's on the Box?

BY PETER COREY

About this book

This book tells the story of TV.

You will need

- *Television KWL grid* Photocopy Master 44, *Teaching Handbook* for Year 2/P3

- *What do I do?* Photocopy Master 45, *Teaching Handbook* for Year 2/P3

	Literacy Framework objective	**Target and assessment focus**
Speaking, listening, group interaction and drama	○ Listen to each other's views and preferences, agree the next steps to take and identify contributions by each group member **3.3**	○ We can express a preference and listen to each other's views and preferences **AF2/3**
Reading See also continuous reading objectives listed on page 9.	○ Explain organizational features of texts, including alphabetical order, layout, diagrams, captions, hyperlinks and bullet points **7.3**	○ We can identify different organizational features that the author has used and discuss why **AF4**

Before reading

To activate prior knowledge and encourage prediction

- Talk to the children about what their favourite television programme is.

- Introduce the word 'preference'. Do they have particular preferences when watching television? For example, do they prefer cartoons or nature programmes?

- Look together at the contents page, ensuring that children know what a contents page is. What sort of book do they think this might be?

- Draw attention to the section title, *Did you know?* Can they predict some facts that might be mentioned?

- Give them the *Television KWL grid* Photocopy Master to fill in with a partner.

To support decoding and word recognition and introduce new vocabulary

- Look at the glossary with the children. Ask them to read the meanings of any unfamiliar words.

- Show them some of the context vocabulary and/or compound and polysyllabic words (see vocabulary chart on p.11). Help them, as necessary, to decode the words and use syntax and context to work out their meaning.

To engage readers and encourage fluent reading

- Read the opening section aloud to the group. (*Switched on*)

- Ask children to read it to each other in pairs, with expression. Caution them not to read on to the next page, until told to do so.

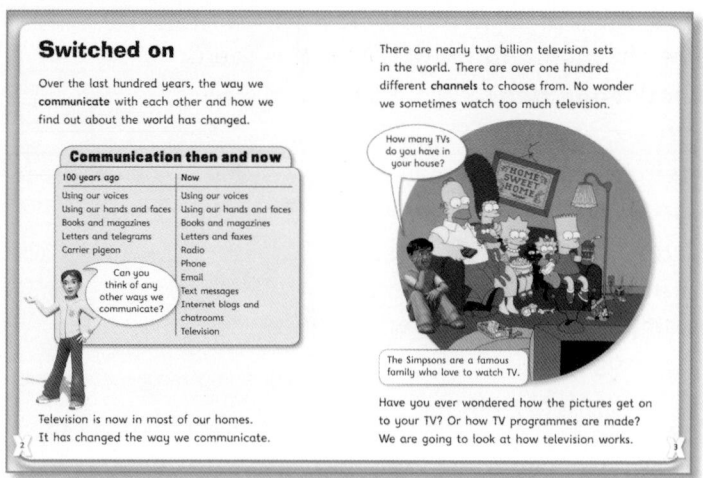

Switched on

Over the last hundred years, the way we **communicate** with each other and how we find out about the world has changed.

Communication then and now

100 years ago	Now
Using our voices	Using our voices
Using our hands and faces	Using our hands and faces
Books and magazines	Books and magazines
Letters and telegrams	Letters and faxes
Carrier pigeon	Radio
	Phone
	Email
	Text messages
	Internet blogs and chatrooms
	Television

Can you think of any other ways we communicate?

There are nearly two billion television sets in the world. There are over one hundred different **channels** to choose from. No wonder we sometimes watch too much television.

How many TVs do you have in your house?

The Simpsons are a famous family who love to watch TV.

Television is now in most of our homes. It has changed the way we communicate.

Have you ever wondered how the pictures get on to your TV? Or how TV programmes are made? We are going to look at how television works.

- Discuss the concept of a billion, providing concrete examples (e.g. a school sandpit probably contains 1 billion grains of sand or more).

 During reading

- Ask the children what to do if they encounter a difficult word, modelling with an example from the book if necessary. Praise children who successfully decode unfamiliar words.

- Ask the children to read the next two sections (*How a TV works* and *Early TV*). What do children notice about the different ways these two sections have been presented? Draw their attention to the use of numbering and blocks of text in the second section (pp.4–7). Then look at the narrative presentation of the third section (p.8). Can they infer why the author has used these two different styles? Which one do they think is most successful? (**activating prior knowledge, adopting a critical stance**)

Assessment point

Can children identify the different organizational features that have been used? AF4

- Read the fourth section (*TV now*) together. How much of the technology are they familiar with? Who has seen or used one of the devices listed? How do they think TV programmes have changed over the years? What are their favourite programmes? (**activating prior knowledge**)

- Focus on the final sentence, and discuss with them what they think will happen in the future of television. (**predicting**)

- Ask them to read to the end of the book independently.

 ## After reading

- Ask children to work as a group and decide on the main points they have learned from the book. (**determining importance**)

- How successful do they feel this book is at putting across information? How do they feel about the book? Can they express a preference? (**personal response, including adopting a critical stance**)

· ·>

Building comprehension

- Ask them to choose the section they found the most interesting and design some questions on the same topic to ask their families at home. (**questioning**)

- Give them the *What do I do?* Photocopy Master. Ask them to write a small paragraph describing what they think each person does, working as a group. (**predicting**)

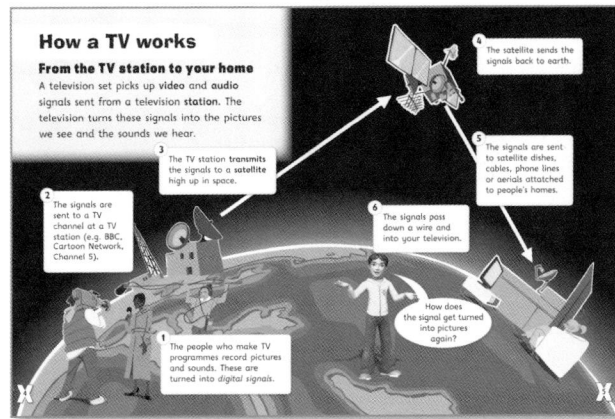

How a TV works

From the TV station to your home
A television set picks up **video** and **audio** signals sent from a television **station**. The television turns these signals into the pictures we see and the sounds we hear.

3 The TV station **transmits** the signals to a **satellite** high up in space.

4 The satellite sends the signals back to earth.

5 The signals are sent to satellite dishes, cables, phone lines or aerials attached to people's homes.

2 The signals are sent to a TV channel at a TV station (e.g. BBC, Cartoon Network, Channel 5).

6 The signals pass down a wire and into your television.

How does the signal get turned into pictures again?

1 The people who make TV programmes record pictures and sounds. These are turned into *digital* signals.

Building fluency

● Reread *Early TV*. What do children know about television programmes that their parents or grandparents used to watch? Encourage them to ask family members what they enjoyed watching and how they compare with programmes of today.

● Ask them to practise reading one of the sections as if they were recording it for (or presenting it in) a documentary programme.

Follow-up activities

Writing activities

● Write a script for a television programme. **(longer writing task)**

● Write a review of their favourite programme. **(longer writing task)**

● Refer the children to the timeline on pages 22 and 23 of the book. Ask them to create a timeline of their lives. **(short writing task)**

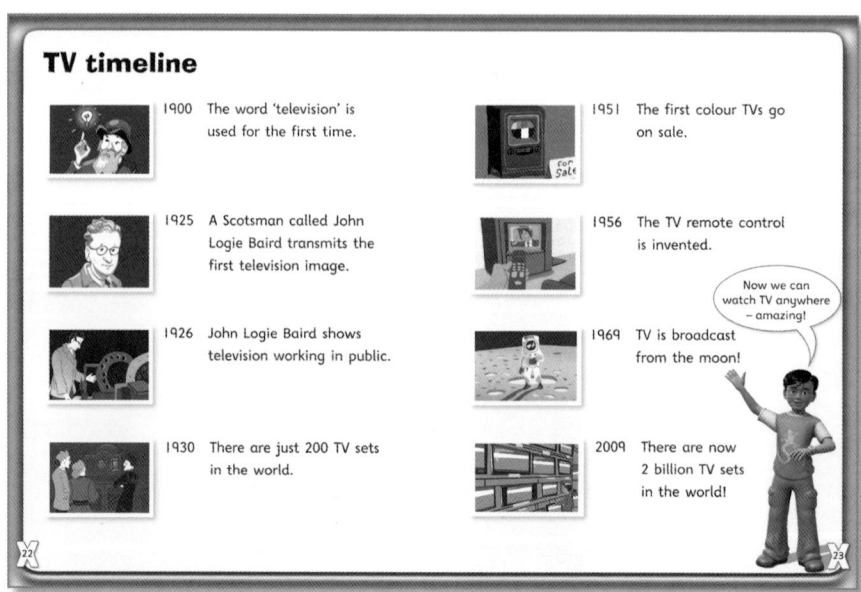

TV timeline

1900 The word 'television' is used for the first time.

1925 A Scotsman called John Logie Baird transmits the first television image.

1926 John Logie Baird shows television working in public.

1930 There are just 200 TV sets in the world.

1951 The first colour TVs go on sale.

1956 The TV remote control is invented.

1969 TV is broadcast from the moon!

2009 There are now 2 billion TV sets in the world!

Now we can watch TV anywhere – amazing!

Other literacy activities

- Talk about (ad lib) a subject for 30 seconds. (**speaking and listening**)

Cross-curricular and thematic opportunities

- Design a questionnaire and carry out a survey about favourite television programmes. (**Mathematics**)
- Research the invention of telephones/television/radio, etc. (**History**)
- Make a television programme. This could be a stop-frame animation using a show box to make a setting or a documentary-style programme with scripts. (**ICT**)
- Create a website to communicate with others. (**ICT**)
- Design a set in a shoe box for a TV programme. (**DT**)
- Look at the work of Seurat (pointillism) and make pictures from dots similar to those seen on TV screens (pp.6–7). (**Art**)

The Deadly Boomslang

BY MICHAELA MORGAN

About this book

This is a traditional African tale, told by a storyteller, about a village terrorized by a deadly snake. The villagers must find a clever way to capture the snake.

You will need

- *Snake words* Photocopy Master 46, *Teaching Handbook* for Year 2/P3

- *Animal sentences* Photocopy Master 47, *Teaching Handbook* for Year 2/P3

	Literacy Framework objective	Target and assessment focus
Speaking, listening, group interaction and drama	○ Tell real and imagined stories using the conventions of familiar story language 1.2	○ We can retell a familiar story to others **AF2**
Reading See also continuous reading objectives listed on page 9.	○ Draw together ideas and information from a whole text, using simple signposts in the text 7.1 ○ Engage with books through exploring and enacting interpretations 8.2	○ We can understand the main facts and events in a text **AF2** ○ We can, with support, begin to predict future events in a story and infer how characters are feeling about themselves and others **AF3**

Before reading

To activate prior knowledge and encourage prediction

- Talk to the children about the tradition of oral storytelling. Discuss how this was different from writing the stories down. Introduce the idea that the stories can change over time. Play 'Chinese Whispers' to focus on how an idea can be changed.

- Ask them if they know what a *deadly boomslang* is, or can suggest what it might be. How could they find out?

- Show them the cover. What types of snake do they know? How do snakes move? What do they eat? Where do they live?

To preview the text

- Take a picture walk through the text. Can children tell the story from the pictures?

- Which part of the world do they think the story is set in? What clues are there to suggest the location? (**deducing**)

To support decoding and word recognition and introduce new vocabulary

- Put some of the new vocabulary words (*Snake words* Photocopy Master) into a cloth bag. Ask children to take out words and work together to decode them as necessary.

- Work together to find the meanings for the words. Then ask children to sort them (e.g. all the verbs together, all the words that begin with 's'). Allow them to explore the different ways that the words might be classified. They might want to make a display of their words, for example on a blank snake outline.

During reading

- If you have not already done so, ask the children what to do if they encounter a difficult word, modelling with an example from the book if necessary. Remind them about the words that you have already collected and displayed.

- Model the reading of the first speech bubble on page 2, ensuring that the children can hear the pattern and rhyme. Ask them to read it back to you in unison.

- Ask them to read to the bottom of page 8.

- Get them to predict who they think will become the leader. (**predicting**)

- Ask them to read to the point where the author is about to reveal what is in the bag (p.19). Can they predict what might be in the bag? (**predicting**)

- Read the rest of the story to them.

· ·>

Assessment point

Can children predict future events in the story? AF3

It was a quiet **hissing** sound.
The boy looked up. He saw a thin, brown-green branch twitch. But it wasn't a branch it was the snake!
It was sliding down the tree now, moving towards the boy. It was swelling up its neck, ready to bite.

The boy slipped his hand into his bag. What did he have?
Was it an axe?
A knife?
A big stick?
No.
It was ...

 **After reading**

Returning to the text

- What did the group notice about how the author said *"... but they didn't even SEE the snake!"* Why is the word *SEE* in capital letters? What does this imply? (**inferring**)

- Ask children to create three different freeze-frame images:
  - the old lady, the boastful boy, and the other villagers
  - the old lady, the second boy, and the villagers
  - the old lady, the villagers, and the quiet boy

  and discuss the relationships between them. (**synthesizing**)

· ·>

Building comprehension

- Can children identify the most important point: that only one boy listened? (**determining importance**)

- Go into role as the old lady. Get children to ask her what she thought about the three boys. (**questioning**)

· ·>

- Ask the children why the first two boys were not successful in catching the snake. (**summarizing**)

- Can children speculate on how they might have captured the snake? (**activating prior knowledge**)

Building fluency

- Ask the children to prepare the two rhymes from the story (one at the beginning and one at the end) for a group performance to the rest of the class.

> **Assessment point**
>
> Can children identify the signposts and main events which enable them to draw conclusions about the relationships between the different characters? (The old lady *muttered*, the first boy *boasted*, the second boy *wasn't listening*, the quiet boy *listened*, etc.) AF2/3

> **Assessment point**
>
> Can children identify how the old lady feels towards the three boys? AF3

- Get them to retell the story to someone else in the class, using the pictures as reference points.

Building vocabulary

- Using pictures of animals, ask children to role-play small animals.

- Provide them with the *Animal sentences* Photocopy Master. Ask them to write short, alliterative sentences around the outlines, modelled on the snake on page 5 of the text. (*It was a silent slithery sly and scaly scary sneaky deadly snake!*)

- Ask them to think of a good word for movement, just as the author has on page 17 (*rushing*, *scurrying*). Get them to try and write the word as a calligram. Display the words in the classroom.

Now at that time there was a problem in the village. This was the problem:

It was a silent slithery sly and scaly scary sneaky deadly snake!

5

Follow-up activities

Writing activities

- Design a fact-file about a boomslang. (**short writing task**)
- Write instructions for making a trap. (**longer writing task**)
- Write their own snake jokes. (**short writing task**)

Other literacy activities

- Ask someone in their family to tell them a story that they can then retell to a group of children. (**speaking and listening**)
- Retell a story of their own from memory, perhaps something that happened when they were younger. (**speaking and listening**)

> **Assessment point**
>
> Can children retell a familiar story? AF2

Cross-curricular and thematic opportunities

- Compare and contrast homes in this text with their own homes. (**Geography**)
- Compare and contrast where the children live with a village, town or city in Africa. (**Geography**)
- Design their own snake traps. (**DT**)

Let's Play and other things animals say

BY ALISON BLANK

About this book

A non-fiction text about the fascinating ways that animals communicate with each other.

You will need

- *Animal summary* Photocopy Master 48, *Teaching Handbook* for Year 2/P3
- *Frog haiku* Photocopy Master 49, *Teaching Handbook* for Year 2/P3

	Literacy Framework objective	Target and assessment focus
Speaking, listening, group interaction and drama	○ Listen to others in class, ask relevant questions and follow instructions **2.1**	○ We can listen to other children describing what they have read and ask relevant questions **AF2**
Reading See also continuous reading objectives listed on page 9.	○ Explain organisational features of texts **7.3** ○ Use syntax and context to build their store of vocabulary when reading for meaning **7.4**	○ We can talk about the different ways in which the author has presented information **AF4** ○ We can use a variety of strategies to work out unfamiliar words **AF1**

Before reading

To activate prior knowledge and encourage prediction

- Read the contents page together. Ask children to act out each chapter heading (e.g. croak like a frog). You may want them to practise this a few times, so that they can create a performance.

- Which other animals can they name? How do those animals communicate?

- Does anyone in the group have animals of their own? How do children communicate with them? How do they know when they are hungry? Or angry? Or happy?

- Play a miming game. Ask children to communicate an emotion through body language and facial expressions. Get others to guess how they are pretending to feel.

To preview the text

- Read pages 2 and 3 together. What other things does the group say most days to different people?

- Can children think of different ways to communicate without words? Give them a few challenges (e.g. 'Let someone know you are hungry without saying anything'). (**sensory responses**)

To support decoding and word recognition and introduce new vocabulary

- Take a picture walk through the text. Focus on the different animals and what they are doing, and introduce some of the words identified in the vocabulary chart (p.11).

- Ask children to skim-read the text and identify unfamiliar words. Help them use decoding strategies to read these words and syntax and context to work out their meaning.

· ·>

- Encourage the children to note down unfamiliar words to display in the classroom.

> ### Assessment point
>
> Can children use decoding strategies to work out unfamiliar words? AF1

During reading

- Ask each child to choose the section that interests them the most to read quietly to themselves. Explain that when they have finished reading you will be asking them to summarize the main points of the section. Use the *Animal summary* Photocopy Master. (**summarizing**)

- When they have fed back the main points to the group, encourage them to ask the rest of the group the question that appears in the blue question box on their chosen page.

- Ask them what they have learned about the different animals. Which methods of communication seem to be most effective? (**adopting a critical stance**)

- Get other children to ask the reader questions about their chosen section. (**questioning**)

- Let the group read any of the sections that have not been covered.

. . . . ➔

Birds strut

Being noticed

Many male birds have spectacular feathers or unusual colours to attract attention.

To **impress** a female, the peacock fans out his tail feathers and struts up and down. His tail has over 200 feathers. Each tail feather is decorated with a beautiful pattern which looks like an eye.

When a peacock shows off his feathers, he is saying "Look at me!"

? *How do you say, "Be my friend"?*

The blue-footed booby gets a female's attention by showing off his handsome blue feet.

After reading

Returning to the text

- Focus children's attention on the different ways of presenting information (e.g. pictures as well as text, rectangular and oval frames, bold print for words in the glossary, blue question boxes to encourage readers to engage with the text, labels on the pictures and captions under them, magnified/cut-out images, the quiz at the end of the book). Talk about how these features and techniques help the reader to engage with and understand the information. Give children time to look at other books and compare the features and techniques used. (**adopting a critical stance**)

··>

> **Assessment point**
>
> Can children talk about how effective they find the different presentational techniques that the author has used? AF4

Building comprehension

- Ask each child to take a turn to be the tour guide for one section. Encourage children to point out the features and techniques that the author has used to involve the reader. Other children could continue to use the *Animal summary* Photocopy Master to record information. (**adopting a critical stance**)
- Ask the children what new ideas or information they have gained from reading the book. (**summarizing**)
- Are there points or pieces of information in the book that they do not understand? (**adopting a critical stance**)

Building fluency

- Once the children have acted as tour guides for their section, ask them to practise reading that section so that they can read it to the group as an expert.

Building vocabulary

- Provide a range of books, websites, magazines, pictures, etc. about animals. Get children to make a collage about a chosen animal.

Follow-up activities

Writing activities

- As a group, write a haiku poem about a frog, using the *Frog haiku* Photocopy Master. The structure of a haiku requires that the first line has 5 syllables, the second line has 7 syllables, and the last line has 5 syllables. To write as a group, each child writes words of one syllable on individual slips of paper. The group then chooses their favourite words (adding up to 17 syllables) and arranges them into a haiku. (**short writing task**)

- Create an A3 non-fiction spread about how a particular animal communicates, making use of features and techniques that encourage the reader to engage with the text. (**longer writing task**)

Other literacy activities

- Read and perform poems about animals and their sounds. (**speaking and listening**)

Cross-curricular and thematic opportunities

- Study different animals and, if possible, observe them in their natural habitats (**Science**).
- Create observational drawings of different animals. (**Science, Art**)
- Try to recreate animal sounds using instruments. (**Music**)